The Ink of Light

Sheila,
To a true
friend and a
wonderful writer!
Thank you for
your love &
encouragement!
Love Trish

Poems by Patricia Abram

White Mountain Publications

WHITE MOUNTAIN PUBLICATIONS
A Division of White Mountain Investments Ltd.

Box 5180
New Liskeard, Ontario
Canada P0J 1P0

Cover Design: Deborah Ranchuk
Cover Photo: Patricia Abram
Author Photo: Susan Ashukian

CANADIAN CATALOGUING IN PUBLICATION DATA

Abram, Patricia, 1958-
The Ink of Light: poems

ISBN: 1-896331-77-7

I. Title.
PS8551.B52154 2000 C811'.6 C00-931008-8
PR9199.3A172154 2000

ISBN: 1-896331-77-7
Printed in Canada

for Sonya
and the most precious gift she offered me

for my three men,
David, Ben, and Timothy,
with love

"Open the eye of truth..."
Bahá'u'lláh

Table of Contents

I *The Ink of Light*

I

The Ink of Light

"Write all that We have revealed unto thee
with the ink of light upon the tablet of thy spirit."
Bahá'u'lláh

The Ink of Light

"In thy soul of love build thou a fire
And burn all thoughts and words entire."
Jalálu'd-Dín Rúmí

A leaf. Its wet flesh on yours
as the sun breaks the lake
into light. Into language
without words.

Through your skin the earth feeds you:
tall grass leaning into your thighs,
stone chiselling your foot to its shape,
moss that imprints you. The tang of pine
drawing the sky green.

Just this moment the loon arches
her throat, her call.
The water folds her sound,
your body touches her music, its long note.
A ladder to another world.

How to write with the ink of light.
The prayer that transcends syllable
to soul.

Invocation

Of beauty.
She tries to find these things.
Of spirit.
In the bark on trees, in the
palms of words.
In green pears. Their flesh,
their scent.
To know this Oneness.

Yet every morning
she struggles to reach
this perfect peace.
Is it hidden under the pages
of daily chores, arguments,
lists that never end?
Or weighed down
by excuses, a refusal to search.

She meditates to find the page,
the language You want,
to dissolve the things of this world.
Once they are gone,
she will open the window
and let the whisper in.
The way a burst of crimson
blooms in a scrap of dying weeds.

Glimpses

Glimpses catch her
in quiet moments,
wind peeling back the leaves,
tongues of poplar yellow in fall

They come as slices of sunlight
across pine needles—a bed of soft rust
They flash as orange in
branches pencil-thin against
blue—a contrast in palette

These perfect moments that
open the eye
shift the landscape
and let the veil of leaves drop
like gold rain

But the wind dies
and she thinks her mind
has caught her in play
created sight where there is no meaning
and she allows the veil to cover the ground
while she walks, brushing aside these glimpses
as though they were dead leaves

Broken Light

As day and night touch, the sky is a puzzle,
pieces of snow-blue
breaking into pockets of light
she finds in her hand,
like a water stain on linen.

Here the trees stand nude
like Greek statues,
female columns naked
under wet drapery that clings,
every curve showing round.
Or not showing.

The trees define a temple
opening into things she can't know.
She lies on her belly,
her face carving an emblem
her hands swimming through snow,
cold swimming through her skin like a river.
She wants to go back
go forward,
carry on without carrying
the things she hides,
the pieces missing, lost in some picture
only she sees.
Her body has forgotten her,
eaten her from the inside,
her nakedness different in new light
she refuses.

She smells burnt umber in the shadows,
the frost that scratches.
Cuts from old wounds buried in her flesh,
slicing through her as if just done.
Her head down, hair scattered as rays on the snow,
she bites herself from praying,

but still the ink of light draws her.

"Love is the ground of all things"
'Abdu'l-Bahá

You break yourself
again and again.
A body held open,
waiting.

As if divine fingers
will fill you with all that you want
without knowing it. That brilliance,
pure as bone, opal in copper earth.

How to mine that vein, this dust in your hand.
To find its wealth, its weight.
To know this mineral love.

Pure Leaven

To loosen myself from this outer skin
like a shadow detaching from bone.
Every dawn the sun brings this moment
and in its rays I cling to the darkness
my body casts.

Knowing there are others, those
symbols who offer up their blood,
their being. These stainless ones,
whose bodies become the bread, the pure leaven
that rises warm for the world, their radiance reflecting
the sun. This earth a mere step they light with
their walk.

To reach the night knowing the bonds I hold,
another day lost in my refusal to shed shadows.
I read Your words, hoping for tomorrow.
The chance to offer my body as bread.

"Consider the human eye"

Bahá'u'lláh

There are days I don't water
the flowers outside in the window boxes.
Days and days. And I know the plants are
dying, their fuchsia petals wilted like
thin scraps of felt. Leaves faded to
amber, a warning.

I turn my eye in another direction,
seeking the solidness in my house,
the flowered carpet in my living room.
It's the perspective I can change,
the angle my eye will allow,
to highlight certain images, shade others.

Just as there are days the water
spills on parched leaves,
bringing moisture to the dark eye
of my humanity.

Iris

Wet fields
and your eyes fall upon
wild iris purple-blue in the grass.
Named for the Greek rainbow goddess,
waving like a fleur-de-lis,
a flag in the sun.
You talk of meanings, appearance
and see things changing—
an iridescent eye,
its coloured curtain contracts,
changing your perception.
How you see rainbows
on water,
mother-of-pearl,
feathers.

A Single Point

In the evening sun
you bring the lake to your mouth
the wind like fingers in your hair,
this reaching

The clouds move you,
shift your place in the sky—
the dock beneath you
            a wooden road one way
white pines another,
a split that lives only in the mind
as reflection

like this illusion in the glass
you are bending to

Mines

"Send down a shaft of light"
'Abdu'l-Bahá

In late summer
the garden runs its own course—
tangles and twists
she had abandoned for things
more important.

A density reigns there
of curled leaves, frenzied weeds
winding through her order,
growing disorder,
neglecting her as she neglected it.

Every spring she spreads the composter's
rich flesh over the garden soil
and every fall
a squash grows unplanned
unplanted,
its leaves shaped like spades,
its orange-yellow flower blooming
a green acorn her son picks
to feed them.

Last night she dreamed of worms,
a tangle of thousands twisting,
her body giving birth to their wet breath.
They stretched into endless roads
buried in her clothes,
hanging like ropes from her damp skin.
In the morning they were gone
till she remembered the garden,
the September dryness,
the thirst of neglect.

Through openings
her hands travel tunnels,
stroking stems back to life,
digging space in the dark—
there
an orange-yellow gem
grows brilliant
in the shaft of light
that finally mines through.

those stones

you step into the stone foundation
crumbling into ruin,
wild asters purple against red sumac
slivering into the azure sky of fall

you gather this purple, a fistful of
feathered stars and slices of sumac flesh
to bring colour to your table later
after you have walked the afternoon into night

these days you search for palettes
scan the fields for new tones, shades,
your eye craving pigment, your hand the texture
of each leaf, petal, breath—
how to know the truth of sunlight
on a body born with thought

what is it that makes you cling to
these old stones, beliefs that have lived
in your skin like ancient ritual without meaning?
days wander these worn trails, the colours
stretch their hues offering

till finally autumn grows
into a landscape created by your steps
a path you tread into meaning

leaving those stones
to dissolve as history
in the shadow of new light

From heart to skin

It's this way every summer twilight:
the cottage verandah—stretched out on a bed,
she waits the end of day,
green leaves becoming grey
        becoming black against night,
a moth powdering the windows with its wings.

Light through the door hinge in a back bedroom.

It's the leaves chanting that keep her still,
        from heart to skin.
A desire to know their words,
unravel their sounds like letters from a scroll,
        tiny parchment wrapped as each curl.

She knows there's listening to be done
        if only her soul would open
like moth wings against black,
or leaves shaking light
        through a hinge.

The Word

Without syllable or sound
        the Word is alive,
                surrounding
She walks the path
        birches bending white velvet in her hands
On the ground a cluster of fungi is a city of caverns
        opening within
Beyond she tries to find the senses for this Word that has no
        form, pervades all elements without element itself

She wants to touch this creative Word that rains grace
        on all things,
this source of Oneness, inspiration
She wants to taste it the way skinless almonds
        slide velvet on her tongue

Balance

The Word is alive,
        surrounding
The scent of milkweed flowers here
as you walk down the same road you always walk down
        afternoons at the cottage
Between trees a thick dog, heavy head on a thick chain,
        clambers and chomps, barks,
teeth white as bone within its muzzle, bristling,
        as you go by every time

You remember its ancestor,
        the three-legged dog
a Rottweiler, as this four-legged one,
remember how it would balance its weight
        perfectly like a scale
as though an invisible force held it in place
Was it born this way, you wondered, a birth defect
        or act of nature?
you remember how the dog would slide its chain
back and forth along the rope
        attached between two pines,
the gasping, choking, to reach you
What would it do if the rope ever broke?
        Taste your skin?

But one summer the dog wasn't there gnashing teeth,
        tugging along the line
Only a pup's bark not as strong
        yet four legs sturdy on the rocky ground
        meshed with moss,
its small neck wrapped in a collar, choking toward you,
snapping and gnawing those white teeth
When you asked,
        the owner outside chopping wood told you
the mother died, told you she was born with only three legs

Today the dog with four legs balances, calling you
        as you walk by where
the smooth bones of a dead turtle, its bleached shell,
        break the edge of the road
tiger lilies in the tall grasses, blue lupines too,

as you watch the sound of water
        break on a hollow boat

The Moon

She sees the moon as a pearl
its lustre on the black waves hinting
these ripples are but One
leading into
leading from the same,
an endless mystery to some,
an easy riddle to others

tonight the moon is
an eye she finds moving within her,
a lake of light
opening

into this truth

into night

you slide into night
        into the black lake in a black sky
and float placeless between two worlds
your face open to the universe

in that moment
you are sky, you are lake
you are neither, you are both,
        the stars breathing as your thoughts

Stillness

There's a stillness in the way the moon rides the lake,
          stars watching, breathless.

At night mice have their way,
          gnawing into your sleep.
A distant howl across the water pulls the day back into focus,
and the constant ping of a bat against the screen awakens
          you to its nocturnal rhythm.

Finally you spurn all this nighttime chatter
and leave the cottage for the end of the dock,
preferring instead to lie under the moon,
          its soundless motion riding you
                    breathless.

paths

paths through the forest
        like veins through your body

there is breathing here
        in the rocks
a slow heaving

rains have slit open the earth's skin
        a kind wound

it is dusk now, the sinking
        of day into night,
the sky muted like a lover's touch

tomorrow waits in a closed bud
        such holy breath

certitude

"The true seeker hunteth naught but the object of his quest,
and the lover hath no desire save union with his beloved."
Bahá'u'lláh

our reunion was wet and close,
light rain gracing the lake and white pines,

You found me there
in the breath between each branch

the sky a shawl
draping us in silver

tall grasses veiled us in
moaning winds, knowing
    the slowness of soft rain

***

Like a silk scarf.
This falling into You.
I have only Your words,
no flesh, but yet
this is flesh.
The very heart of You in
each syllable, sound
held on my tongue.
Becoming a language that
collapses words
into an end that knows no end.

This blessing drifts
silk in the sky.

breaths, blessings

1.

breaths, blessings
as a sigh from the one sun
that warm stone
a circle within a circle within

know that all spokes radiate
from this one hub, roll through
this field   You see how this language
tells all   hides all
You give it from Your tongue
I take it on mine

2.

my soul becomes a map for Your words
a geography with traces of Your touch
I struggle to find the poetry Your lips know
spoken without sound

3.

You speak in metaphor
bend words like these long grasses
in this field   wrap them into crowns
anointing us with Your grace

our thoughts dissolving
in Your breath

is light, is song

listen how light becomes song
its brightness ringing
its dimness humming

see how song becomes light
the notes lifting into vision
beyond sound

Your text is light I hear
is song I see
my eyes and ears vanishing
as words

hidden words

"Immerse yourself in the ocean of My
words that ye may unravel its secrets..."
Bahá'u'lláh

within each passage
there lies a pearl
opulent in its roundness
an emerald in this quote, a sapphire as
blue star in this line

treasures to be mined
over and over into memory into mind
this chanting of cerebral chords

without words we speak
the language of the soul,
a holy syntax, free from
the body of sound

in this stillness
like glass in water becoming one
I hear Your voice answer and

my tongue, my pen, my whole being, testify

Without Weight

I imagine You
as an amber leaf
            wind chiming the trees
this leaf a yellow flame
            one perfect flicker
            that falls from the sky
            without weight.

I imagine You
as the smell of grass
the triangle roof top
            slate-grey in the afternoon sun
            these angles all around me.
The crimson berries
            I would bring to my mouth.

You are all these
You are none.
Like air in the cup of my hand.

reading the light

she wants to read the bark on trees
          a river's current
          the story of a loon's call

late summer
her back rests on the grass
          this hard earth
the smell of pears and roses
Manitoba maples splayed above her
her body becomes the blue sky
          opening

light as ink
writes between each leaf
          each leaving

Liquid Light

Smell rain
its wet hand on the earth's back
Peel off life's skin
and slide into this cleansing sliding into

The lake takes you deep within,
liquid light, an ink printed on this clear face
your body touches each invisible word
your mouth holds each meaning

you want to write of the pearls
hidden within the rain

Visions

Driving through morning light
a lace of mauve sweeps the field
the oars of rowers split the lake
stroke after stroke
into a vision pushing forward
as she returns home along this road.

There is a tenderness to this light
shy in its offering like two hands
opening with a bright treasure
unsure of the value but offered
with hope, humility.
It is the way the light strokes the glass,
the seat, her legs, hands on the wheel.
A warm grace. And she pushes on
into a landscape that will change
with each moment, the light splitting
her vision of time
shifting scenes
into night.

To Perfect Peace

To perfect peace.
In this dusk,
you find threads silver—
a spider's script on lilac leaves, its scent
stays as memory, meaning lost.

How to know this:
the word for Being.
Becoming. Always becoming
the true self. To know this.
As a child's head falls back
to catch the water in his hair, the root of
a mother's hand growing within.
See the language wet on the thin strands—
naming
          over and over.

naming

"The enlightenment of the world of thought comes from these centers of light and sources of mysteries. Without the bounty of the splendor and the instructions of these Holy Beings the world of souls and thoughts would be opaque darkness."

'Abdu'l-Bahá

the sun shed its light, its skin
and draped this mantle on a few
who walked throughout history
unfolding this holy garment.
all named by the source, named the same
though wearing different language.
their words tell the same story
in different clothing,
if eyes open and see.
let the sun open you
pour light as skin into you
over you. illumine you
with this bright ink.

Moses, Krishna, Zoroaster, Buddha,
Christ, Muhammad, the Báb, Bahá'u'lláh

the rays of one Light

II

Women Bear Witness to the Light

(A Suite of Dramatic Monologues)

Old Woman at the Sea

I was there, I was.
Saw him, his beard raging like a river,
that rod in his hand, arm raised in the air,
the sea parting like a split reed
as we clamored in droves behind him.
He had that fiery look in his eye, I tell you,
like the time he came down from
the mountain, his face all aflame
like the Burning Bush that spoke to him
and gave him the Word to follow.

Oh this Moses showed us the way, led us
out of Egypt, but his heart never landed in Canaan
with the rest of us. We eat our matzah
and bitter herbs, no leaven in the house,
to remind us of the hard times in Pharaoh's
land, our flight.

And we tell the story of Exodus
on this night that is different from
all others: the sea bending, dividing
to his Word.

Mother of the Pandavas Speaks of the Light

I knew it was he who had saved us, by his grace,
saved us from the fire, my five sons and I.

When he rode into the city as a royal prince
and came to me in yellow robe, his body smeared
with sandalwood, a necklace of Kaustubha jewels
circling garlands of flowers, I knew

it was more than just my nephew who kneeled
and touched my feet. My eyes wet, I embraced
Lord Krishna,

his touch waking me like a lotus-flower open to light—
my face smiling spiritual bliss, worldly concerns
fell away from me like dead petals dropping,

my senses blessed with life, blazing, as though I had
awakened from a long sleep.

My voice choked as I told him I knew
he would always keep us safe by his grace
as he was always seated in our hearts,
his light in all,

and I knew it was I who should kneel
and touch his lotus feet.

Old Maidservant Speaks at Prince Vishtasp's Palace

Now Farshad, you were in the Master's stable
tending to the camels—so you don't know.
Now me, I was there. Tending to the fire,
rolling rice in olive leaves. Then that knock,
a gentle one, hard to tell at first if someone was
there. Jasmine, that young maid-girl with the
doe eyes and pouty lips, tugged open the palace door,
and me, I peeked around the corner and saw him.
Matted hair and a tattered robe he had, grizzled beard.
He demanded to see the Prince, had a message
to share.

Our Master welcomed this wanderer with open
arms, gave him the finest silk pillow to sit on
and asked me to bring some wine and dates.
I heard his name was Zoroaster, and that he was
a prophet of the one True God.

Now don't look at me like that, Farshad,
that's what he said, and I believe him.
It's the light in his face, his voice,
such a holy weight, though no one
has listened to his words yet, he said.

He told the Prince of his seven visions
of the Sacred Fire and his conversations
with this one True God who sees
into the hearts of all, speaks of
the choice that lies in our hands.
He spoke and the Prince listened,

and I listened too, Farshad,
and his Good Religion has spread.

A Woman Looks Back at a Day by the Stream
528 BC

I was kneeling by the stream, dipping my clay jug,
when I saw him. At first I thought

it was a dead carcass, skin weathered and bleached
by the sun, bottle-green flies picking at bones,
but when I ran to his side I saw that frail cage
of his chest rise and fall so slowly. His head

in my lap, pale against my saffron-coloured sari,
I brought drops of water to his parched lips, slid
grains of rice onto his tongue, and he took them.
He told me he had fasted, searching through

austerity, but he learned that was pointless.
His friends, disgraced by his failure, left him,
but he let them go, and under the spreading
branches of that sacred fig tree

the veil lifted and he awoke to light.
I was there in Deer Park when he spoke
of the Eightfold Path and over the years
I followed it, as the Buddha wandered the Ganges,
spreading the Truth.

A Young Woman in the Market

I saw him in the temple that day
when his mother went looking for him
fearful he was lost.
He was a boy of twelve,
but there on his brow
was the weight of hundreds, nay
thousands upon thousands of souls, yet
a sweetness like the mangos I held in my hands
blossomed on his face, as I made my way
through the market, wondering who he was.

Years later I saw a man
standing on a mount, heard his words,
and I knew he was the boy in the temple,
his face a sun above the sky,
I wanted to bend at his feet, hide my face
in his robes, but he bid me look at him
and I saw the light John spoke of
when the dove descended upon
this Jesus in the river Jordan.

On that mount he prayed to wash
from me the dust of this earth.
From there I followed this Christ, his word,
his way, to the cross he carried on his back
through the narrow streets, carrying with him
the weight of all those souls.

Old Woman Speaks on her Deathbed to a Maidservant

619 AD

I remember the day I first saw him among the traders,
lush carpets, silks and sugars among his wares,
a pensive look on his sweet face.

They called him *al-Amin*, the trusted one, his honesty
so open on his sleeve I asked him to handle my affairs,
I a rich widow then, you know, he fifteen years younger,
though I could see the wisdom in those eyes and
offered him my hand to wed, and lo! my pleasure
when he accepted, a man of only five and twenty.

Did you know his father died before my blessed one
was even born, and his mother, may Allah bless her soul,
died when he was only six. Such a life! And he illiterate.

But he had the searching way, and after
talks of faith in places far and wide,
he withdrew to a mountain Cave
outside that holy city of Mecca.
Gave himself wholly to prayer.

One night he burst into the house
where I was having tea and dates,
his face all flushed, blazing like a crimson light, sobbing
that Angel Gabriel had come to him in his trance and said,
'*Recite! Recite in the name of thy Lord*' and he
had awoke with those words inscribed upon his heart.

Many more visions came, the words streaming forth,
held to memory, then later passed to others
who wrote on palm-leaves, stones, anything at hand.

But I tell you now, as I am readying to meet my Lord,
after Ali, I was the first to follow Muhammad,
the first to follow his sacred words.

Old Woman on the Rooftop, July 9th 1850

Masoud, I know. I tell you, my son, I know of
what I speak, I was there on the rooftop that day.
You were off on some caravan, making greedy trades
under the hot sun, your sweat like rivers on your face,
how could you possibly know?

Yes, yes, I know I closed my ears to this one
who called himself the Báb, his message spreading
through Tehran like fire, through all of Persia.
But that was before the day on the rooftop.

How was I to know that a youth from Shíráz, a mere
merchant in a green turban could be a prophet of God?
Proclaiming a new day, that he was the Gate to another
far greater *who shall ere be made manifest.*
I tell you, there were some who would give up their lives
for him, those who swore to the light in his face,
his soft manners like silk on skin.

These faithful ones hugged the rooftop, there with me,
some weeping, others wailing, I couldn't understand why.
Till I saw him. His soulful eyes, two black jewels
blazing a treasury of light to those who could truly see.

What was his crime? Why was this one to die?
My son, I think those in power could read
the truth in his eyes, and knew they had to douse it
to save their own command. They tied this one, the Báb,
to a spike in a pillar, suspended him with rope, another
youth beside him in that courtyard of two hundred and fifty
poised with guns.

The sound, such a roar, and the smoke, the sky unseen,
those bullets a brutal shower, but lo! my astonishment
when the smoke lifted like a veil, and there stood
the other youth unscathed, ropes torn,
and that one, the Báb, nowhere to be seen.

I swear to you, Masoud, he was nowhere to be seen.
They found him back in his cell, finishing his last task on this earth,
then consented to their wishes, walking back to that courtyard,
ready to offer up his body, his blood.

Masoud, my son, the clock struck noon, the shots blazed out,
then a whirlwind of dust blackened the sky as though midnight
had fallen on us all, and I tell you, we saw no sunlight
from noon till night that day.

The bodies of the two youths twined, their flesh and bone
mangled, mingled as one, but their faces untouched,
a smile on the Báb's lips
I carry that light with me
to this day, Masoud.

Old Woman Remembers her Time in the Garden

April 21, 1863

I remember roses, my sweet child, the scent of roses.
Every dawn gardeners would pick them,
heap them in mounds on the Persian rug in his tent.
So hard to see our beloved over the fan of petals
as we drank tea, drinking in his holy presence.

Many came—nobles, the poor and outcast—
this blessed Beauty leaving Baghdad,
lavishing alms as he neared the Tigris,

crossing the river to the Garden, and staying twelve days,
the waves of friends swelling in to bid farewell
to this wronged one who was to be exiled yet again
to another land. You shake your head, my child.
I know, sweet Mina, how could this be true?
This one who only wanted peace, now sent away.
But lo! the joy when on that first day
he declared the Light of his true self, as the one
made manifest. And this garden now known
as *Ridván*, and this day the most holy day.

Years later nearing his death in that prison-city 'Akká,
he wrote of his revelation during the dark days in the Black Pit,
a most dank dungeon in the lowest depths of Tehran,
thrown there ten years before he reached the Garden,
galling chains a hundred pound weight on his neck,
his feet in stocks, hundreds of souls crowded, breathing
a stench the most loathsome to be known.

Here in a dream the Most Great Spirit, as Luminous Maiden
of light, touched his brow. And something flowed from the crown
of his head over his breast, every limb of his body set afire,
his tongue reciting what no man could bear to hear.

My sweet child, Bahá'u'lláh's light touched my soul
and I followed him in exile,
breathing the holy fragrance of his beauty.

III

The Body of the World

The Body of the World

"tell of the blowing of the spirit of life
into the body of the world"
'Abdul'l-Bahá

Under the night sky,
black like the pupil of an eye
watching me,
I meditate on the stirring of stars,
the long-ago sculpting of clay orbs
that broke into colours, some
burning red, others spinning ice,
diaphanous rings.
Our globe spiralled into rivers
stretching like veins
to oceans pregnant with souls.

Yesterday the wind blew breath
into the sand like a mother's cord
pulsing life into her womb.
My sons tunnelled the lake—
goggles as their eyes,
flippers as their feet
transforming them
into amphibian ancestors.
Licked sleek by water
and born into sun
they crawled onto land,
their limbs sucking the shore,

light sighing from their skin.

november

for David

it's november and you pull out the impatiens,
their petals frozen thin against the sidewalk
as though pressed flat in a book, a sad memory
of something forgotten.
you rake the stray leaves curled in the bushes,
holding onto branches, struggling against the wind.
you keep the collar of your coat up around your face—
I can see only your dark eyebrows, continuous,
stretching like one long road across your forehead,
your green eyes looking elsewhere.

they see the lake last summer,
the table outside the cottage and the fondue
we are trying to light that is already lit, though
we can't tell because the wind keeps blowing.
they see the oil being poured again and the flame
burning up your arm, your shirt, the hair on your neck,
you running to the clothesline to smother it in towels
in the scatter of our screams till you realize
the fire is burning our son's head. it won't stop as you
slap his hair, till you plunge him in the lake.
your eyes see the road to the hospital, his cries searing
your skin, the second, third degrees burns wrapped in gauze,
his face a sterile white reminder. your burns minor,
gone in a day.

at night our son sweats the summer heat
and your eyes look elsewhere as you slip into
the cool of the lake, thinking about a day in november
when you'll rake leaves and remember a scar
that burns still.

Rising
for David

In the dark you leave me,
your spine arcing silver in
the grey light that spies through our window.
I feel you as a murmur, a shadow detaching
from bone, fading into light faint as ash.
Sense you slipping into your running pants,
the stretch of their snugness against your thighs.
You try not to wake me, try to miss the creaks in the floor,
tender pine bruised by our daily lives.

When the door clicks shut,
I wrap the blankets into my skin and
think of you on the street,
your legs stretching the sidewalk,
your breath chanting a rhythm
leaving mist in the air, your print on the landscape,
vanishing.

You run through the portal between night and day,
opening into full stride, passing others in windows,
their lives closed in sleep,
and I wonder what drives you day after day
to rise in the shadows
and bound through the dark
like a deer, hunted, tearing through trees,
your body smelling of sweat
as you slide in beside me,
your taste of salt quivering on my lips.

Your Own

for Ben

Through woods and words:
the two paths merge in you,

the one your feet pound day after day
following your father's footsteps
through trees, afternoon sun,
this passion running
born of blood, his seed.

I see his stride in your strong legs,
though your stamp shouts like a signature
sewn on your chest, announcing selfhood.

The other, your eyes take
running over pages, poetry or prose,
this gift I offer of books, words
born of blood, my heart.

I see my style in your lines,
though your pen runs across the page
through afternoon sun, writing your own story.

Through words and woods,
your own path unfolds.

piano
for Timothy

afternoon light
sprawls across the piano
as his fingers sprawl across the keys
his body swaying with the music he creates
this world of sound fashioned from his hands
becoming ivory

his skin sings to the poem
glinting from his fingers
that light hovering as aura in
harmony with aureole

measure for measure
his hands are the keys
to his spirit
offered here
in grace

A Motion Still

I remember your blue hat, netted veil
catching the brown of your bangs
and your white gloves gripping a patent purse,
mint chiclets you chewed in our white pontiac,
the rituals of sundays.

the children's room sighed a closet of
secrets and supplies   stencils and crayola,
cracks tracing the wall and
my grandmother teaching the word,
her grey hair curled into knots, her cat glasses
pointing out her fierce love for Jesus.

you perched on the pew,
your ancestry backing the family view,
your hands folded in disbelief
till the charade stopped when I was six and
we slept in sundays.

you meditate the cancer globed in your breast,
a stillness in motion.
you tell me that flux, fire, live in twig and blade,
stone and cedar, flesh,
beginning in the cell that motions   still
beyond the stencils and crayola and cracks,
a secret past the pew

and you motion still.

Nests

Last year
under our evestrough
a blue jay carved a nest
on a criss-cross of wires
connected to our house.
The bird gathered curls
of leaves, sticks, twists of hair,
grass. Wound them into a
circle. Finally she sat
on eggs I imagined to be
ovals of smooth yellow.
She'd fly away to collect food
for herself,
or her babies—
I wasn't sure if they were born yet.

My mother waits for the birth
of cancer from breast to bone.
Or brain.
Feeling an ache in her pelvis,
dizziness in her head.
She scratches out her concern
through telephone wires,
her worries nested to herself,
now to me.

Pears grow every August on
an ancient tree in our backyard
and every year the squirrels
gnaw them into orbs of cheek.
Last June as I pulled weeds in the garden
a squirrel slunk across
that wire link,
ate the globes of egg,
transparent bird flesh.

This spring my son
tells me of construction.
Another building.
He points to a nest
balancing on the same wires,
points to tail feathers striking blue
above the twigs.
We watch
as the bird gathers,
sits, waits the days.
Waits.

Today the nest curls alone.
I look for the squirrel
and know the circle curves—
in August
pears will fester
like tumours
in closed mouths.

Her Light

for my mother

"Within every blade of grass are enshrined
the mysteries of an inscrutable wisdom."
Bahá'u'lláh

My mother has cancer,
a stone in her breast they dug up,
its fine grains seeping to her blood.
Every day she sews stitches
creating quilts,
one for each grandchild,
seven in all.

She cups the cancer in her hand
like an orb of clay,
and meditates on its light.
On the phone she tells me
how she flows into its shine,
leaving her body like a wisp of dried skin.
How she sinks into peace,
soft palms lifting her, the light an eye
encircling her. For ten minutes, an hour,
she travels this ray and lands like a sigh,
full, unbroken.

This light burns, she says,
in the veins of a girl with auburn hair,
in every man creased with age,
in blades of green that slit the sky.

With fingers stiff, she sews her days,
her thread stitching light
into each quilt.

Spells

in memory of Alberta Irving Lennox

The window outlines her shock
of grey hair, head shaking,
hands flitting like wings,
hitting spirits not there
as my mother struggles to pour
sugared orange juice down her mother's throat.

Outside the night smells of earth and moss,
slugs trailing yellow across my skin.
Outside, my mother ordered,
your grandmother's having one of her spells.
Too little sugar in her blood,
too much insulin sliding in her veins.
Shot by her morning needle.

Once she showed me her marks—
bruises blue like a thunder sky
in the flesh of her arm,
hills smeared purple on her thighs
and rivers streaming yellow down her belly.
Said her body looked like a pastel picture.

When the reaction spread through her
she had been reading my tea cup,
spilling out my future from
the shape of leaves,
sliding into a different spell—
the magic she speaks.

Within the window's light
my mother holds her mother,
holds the empty glass,

and voices speak through open screens.

His Hands

in memory of Howard Lennox

He sits at the table
his plate before him,
the fork built-up,
foam on the handle.
Still, almost too hard to hold.
So much to hold:
He remembers the paint brush
thin in his hand
leaves of autumn orange, gold
curling from its tip,
rivers sliding down his canvas
the sweep of azure sky, his creation.
Remembers the afternoon lake and
the sleek bass wet in his hands,
so much life beneath those scales,
the struggle.
Remembers his fingers on ivory
smooth like warm stone
his movements precise and intimate,
he knows this music
as in his soul.

This Christmas my son serenades him
with songs on his keyboard,
offers the instrument to him as gift.
His ancient fingers fumble, trip,
they want what his mind still has.
He does not know this skin
that holds him now.

In the hospital
a machine marks his beat,
his daughters hold his hands,
they speak of love, this leaving
and meeting her again.
His heart stops the weariness.
And as he sheds his earthly skin,
his hands become music.

Octobers

for my aunt

My mother's sister walks a different life,
her legs twisted from birth.
At seven months full with child
my grandmother tripped, fell and
scraped her knee,
blood seeping through the mesh of her hose,
bearing my aunt on a bloody bed.
In the kitchen sat a four-quart
basket of October apples,
her two-pound body was wrapped
in cotton rags, tucked in that basket
and shoved in the oven.
That's what saved her, the doctors said.
Though she knew it was God.

My grandfather tucked
hot water bags beside her,
took a taxi to the hospital,
the wooden basket on his knee,
the ride fifty cents.
Every day my grandmother walked
to give suck to her infant doll,
then she squeezed her big breasts
stretched full like a cow's udder,
to collect bottles of sweet milk
that fed the twins of a mother
whose dugs had bled dry.

Thighs turned in, my aunt walked on her toes,
her tendons pulled tight
till she had her legs sliced open,
metal plates shoved in and a body cast
to set her in place.
She suffered the operation twice,
the muscles in her thighs so strong
they split the steel blades.

Years later a storm struck
our cottage weekend
as we ate Thanksgiving dinner,
October leaves twisting orange and red.
She sat at the head of the table,
her legs tangled near a brass floor lamp,
rain seeping through the mesh of the closed screen.
Lightning struck the brass pole,
the shock connecting with her blades
twisting like wire through her legs.
Her orthopaedic shoes touched
rubber to the floor.
That's what saved her, my mother said.
Though my aunt knew it was God.

Silver Moon
for my father

Two weeks ago it was my father's
birthday. For sixty-five years
he's touched the earth.
Though he almost died two years ago
as a doctor by-passed his heart
with long-legged veins bridging
knots that clogged his blood.
We had a party to celebrate the luck
of catching time, of wrapping it like a wad of bills
in his fist, shoved in his pocket.

A helium balloon of silver still hangs
in our house. Red letters announcing his years.
One morning I find it in the living room,
touching the ceiling, its blue ribbons
trailing like a stream, a fall of holy water.
In the afternoon it breathes in the family room.
My sons tug on its ties, pull it into their bodies,
crushing it, trying to push out the mysterious spirit
that lets it live, lets it rise.
But it floats undaunted, upward.

After two weeks, I see it near a window,
hovering in the night, free of the ceiling, hanging
like a silver moon, low, the ribbons moving
to silent music, walking in time, as though holding
onto an old man, guiding him through the dark.
The others sleep. I sit on the floor and watch
the globe shrink in a slow sag, losing shape,
its breathless form turning
again and again,
with soundless poise,
with timeless grace.

Valeska Arriving

in memory of Evdokiya Warwaruk Abram,
the grandmother I never knew

I meditate on your passport as though it were a family icon.
Your health certificate outlines your status in
cold letters on a pink card:

> Bathed on March 2, 1923. Baggage disinfected.
> Deloused, vaccinated and examined for venereal
> diseases.

The words tell their story.
Tell me yours.

Woman has big arms, scar like rope. She smell of lye and smoke, shove me in water, coarse fingers scrub my breasts, thighs. Her nails in my hair, hard.

Doctor take me. Lay me on cold table, spread my legs wide. I close my eyes, think of cows at home, calves wet and red, squirming out of that place. His fingers touch me, push me in place no man touch, where blood flow. "What you doing, what you doing?" I sob Ukrainian words he not hear. His face close, breath on my skin. *Mama* back in old country, what she think of me? This man touching me there. I squirm, struggle. He push me down. Push fingers more. Then turn away. He bring back tube with long sharp metal that look like *Mama*'s embroidery needle. He wipe my arm with cloth. It cool like *Tato*'s vodka if it splash on my hand as I pour in cup. That man grab my arm tight, raise sharp point. No, I cry, pull away. He slap me, squeeze my arm and jab needle. My arm sting like time *Tato*'s bees escape from hive and bite me all over legs. But no honey to lick my wound. Only doctor sign his name, stamp my card, stamp me clean.

Tato - father

the myth of eggs
for my father

you slid into this life,
this light,
like yolk sliding from
its shell, the roundness
of the world-egg
breaking open
to possibility.

in Ukraine it is said
the world's fate depends upon
the making of *pysanky*—
if eggs are not dipped
and decorated each year,
we will cease to exist.

an ancient creature lies chained
to a cliff. I imagine it with arms
swarming like snakes, tongue
licking stars from the sky,
skin creased with a map
of the world—erupting, dividing.

the creature's servants circle
the earth like string,
counting the number of eggs
dyed and etched into art.
when numbers are low
the chains loosen and evil spills
like a slick oil,
when numbers are high,
the chains tug tighter—love
choking evil.

I imagine the grandmother
I never met, her round body,
Slavic shape of face,

her farmer's hand
holding your four-year-old hand
days before she left you and your sister,
your father, to slip into her lover's arms,
his house of trinkets and offers.

I imagine her lips sucking the yellow
from the egg,
her thick fingers holding the *kistka*,
writing melted wax on the clean shell,
designing her story in lines, symbols,
dyeing colours, over and over
trying to change the shade, the truth,
after her daughter died of pneumonia,
after she tried to take you back and returned
you, her lover feeding you fish, the bones
stuck in your throat, crying words you couldn't find.

I imagine her dyeing egg after egg,
changing the script, the symbols,
piling the *pysanky* around her like a nest,
her thin shell cracking, her lover taking her
to an asylum where doctors give her medicine,
year after year, till he leaves her there,
forgotten, tied to her story.

I slide into this life,
this light,
broken to the possibility
of having a grandmother, being told she is dead,
while she dyes eggs day after day,
trying to tighten the chains
till she dies in life and I learn of it
twenty years later,
and imagine her lips touching
the smooth clean shell,
imagine her sucking
the bright yellow from the inside.

The Day

in memory of Evdokiya Warwaruk Abram

What was it like the day
they took you away,
flew you on a plane
in a sky you had never known,
or was it a train, chugging the miles
through city to rocks, tracks cut through trees
sliding green outside your window

to a land up north, to a place tucked away,
as they tucked you away in a ward,
leaving you to live years you tried to forget,
the son and daughter you gave away,
a mother's sin.

What was it like that day?
Did they wrap you in white, tying you
to resignation, lost in their string of English words,
your head slung in final defeat?
Or did you go with hat on head, hands folded,
humming some Ukrainian song
or reciting Shevchenko's poems, his call to
remember the words of your mother tongue?

What was it like that day
leaving life behind, did you call out to your
living son or buried daughter or the husband
you left, or the man you ran to, the one
who offered trinkets and houses, the one who left
you to electric shock and revolving doors, the one
who left you to be taken away on a day like this?

Breaking Bread

in memory of Yakiv Abram, the grandfather I never knew

"To Ukrainians, bread is one of the holiest of all foods."
Traditional Ukrainian Cookery

1. Ukraine, 1910

Children sit at desks, Yakiv hides in wheat fields,
stalks swaying yellow on his face, on his sweat,
away from the hours the teacher made him kneel
on the classroom floor of dirt, his knees pressed on
rice she scattered there, the grain printing his skin
with words he couldn't read, couldn't write.

He hides the earth in his hands, the language of his soil,
knows his mother grinds grain at home, her fingers
cut with lines. Knows she bakes bread on a fire,
the door set open in summer heat or winter cold.
A house with no chimney, no windows for escape.

2. The Things I was Told:

My *Dido* loved to sing, but was always off-key,
the notes filtering through his cigarettes, pressed lips.
Years later his round belly rolled out of tune, the lines
in his face playing in time with time. He couldn't read
or write in his mother tongue or the words of his new land,
but relatives who knew him, tell me he was a wise man, born
with a way of knowing, owning the sense that is in the bone
and needs no language to let it sing.

Maybe it was in his hands, like baskets
held open, offering bread. Or maybe
it was in his music, the song of a man hiding,
waiting to find the right voice.

Dido - grandfather

a simple reading

poplars in sunlight talking

a woman bends to her basket
strings her laundry across the sky

her white skirt dances without legs
flutters open like a letter

her hands smell of soap
sweat in the creases of her blouse
she opens to this holy breath
singing

in every act

through the window
sunlight paints glassware blue
steam rising like prayer
as water rolls into vapour
apricots ripen the sill

she lifts the long strands of pasta
soon to be lazy in heat
stirs them into her day

at night
moonlight paints another window
its lunar ink writing secrets on her spine
bent as though in blessing

in a dream, this light

"One of the created phenomena is the dream. Behold how many secrets are deposited therein, how many wisdoms treasured up, how many worlds concealed."
Bahá'u'lláh

"For when the true lover reacheth to the presence of the Beloved, the sparkling beauty of the Loved One and the fire of the lover's heart will kindle a blaze and burn away all veils and wrappings. Yea, all that he hath, from heart to skin, will be set aflame, so that nothing will remain save the Friend." Bahá'u'lláh

there are times all that she needs
finally rises in a dream—
something settles in the mind
quietly like a nudge,
or perhaps flames up, burning

in a dream
the light from those perfect Eyes
fell into her the way fiery liquid falls
from a height

this light moved within her
outward from her heart
though her skin could not hold it,
those holy rays spreading
from all angles of her frame

in a dream,
this light breathed within her,
the split becoming a single One,
this light a sun
though it did not blind her
when she looked

in a dream, this light
upon waking seemed to leave,
though these perfect Eyes
have never left her

Form is a veil

her hair is down to her waist,
the colour of straw,
or sunlight

her eyes the colour of bark
or wet sand

her belly round with the years
of childbirth gone
her hands showing rivers,
or blue streams

her back still straight in yoga poses
or arching in prayer,
legs strong like a bow
or scissors

waiting to be cut from these ties,
the weights that hold her soul

Journey to the Bahá'í House of Worship

"The death of self is needed here, not rhetoric:
Be nothing, then, and walk upon the waves."
Jalálu'd-Dín Rúmí

in the garden
birds sing *a capella* to the landscape
yellow tulips like suns themselves, or stars
their pointy ends bursting fire
it's here I write

of the inside
the temple's silence
watched by an eye, the Word, soaring
high up in the stone lace that
lets the ink of light spray upon me
broken in prayer

that heaviness lost now
in sacred breath

it's here I write
of the self I leave
as old skin
a wisp now vanished
as I step outside, walk
across those waves of grass,
reach for the almond blossoms
soaring

my words on the page as nothing

NOTES ON THE TEXT

Moses - (13th century BC) Hebrew prophet of the Jewish faith, and liberator of Israel. Established Mosaic Law with the Ten Commandments he received on Mount Sinai from Jehovah. Born in Goshen, a part of ancient Egypt. The story of his life is set forth in the Old Testament books of Exodus and Deuteronomy.

Krishna - the eighth avatar of the god Vishnu in the religion of Hinduism. An avatar is the descent of a god into the world of human beings for the duration of a human life span. Hinduism originated in India about 1500 BC. Krishna speaks of love and light, unity and oneness, and the spiritual struggle of the soul in *The Bhagavad Gita*, an ancient Sanskrit poem written in 500 BC.

Zoroaster - prophet-founder of Zoroastrianism. Born in the eastern Persian land of Airyana Vaejah. Dates of his birth and death vary between 630 - 550 BC and six hundred years earlier. He meditated on the nature and origins of good and evil, the concept of free will, and had conversations with Ahura Mazda, the Lord of Wisdom, the One True God. His difficulties spreading the Good Religion are recorded in the Gathas, part of the sacred scripture known as the *Avesta*. Prince Vishtasp of Chorasmia (now in Western Turkistan) was the first to truly champion this faith, after which time the religion spread.

Buddha - (563 - 483 BC) prophet-founder of Buddhism. Born in Kapilavastu, India, which is now in Nepal. His given name was Siddhartha Gautama and he was born into a life of nobility and luxury, but he left that life of self-indulgence in search of enlightenment. In 528 BC he experienced the Great Enlightenment, which revealed the way of salvation from suffering, and gave his first sermon in Deer Park near Benares, expounding the Four Noble Truths and the Eightfold Path, part of the Pali Canon, Buddhist scripture.

Christ - (between 8 and 4 BC - 29 AD, approximate dates) prophet-founder of Christianity. Born in Bethlehem in Judea. Jesus was divinely conceived by Mary. The Gospels in the New Testament are the source of information concerning Jesus' life. His teachings, stressing the infinite love of God and a promise of salvation and eternal life in heaven to all those who repent and follow his way, were offered in his Sermon on the Mount.

Muhammad - (570 - 632 AD) prophet-founder of Islam, the faith of Muslims. Born in Mecca, he belonged to a poor but respected clan, the Hashims, part of the Quraysh tribe. At age twenty-five, he married his first wife, Khadijah. In 610 AD he experienced a vision of the archangel Gabriel who proclaimed Muhammad a prophet of God. He accepted his prophetic mission and preached to the people his belief in one transcendent God, reciting the verses of his revelation, which became known as *The Qur'án*.

The Báb - (1819 - 1850 AD) prophet-founder of the Bábí Faith. Born in Shíráz, Persia on October 20, 1819. His given name was Siyyid 'Alí-Muhammad, and he took the name "Báb" which means "Gate" or "Door" in Arabic. In 1844 he announced that he was a prophet of God and a herald (the Gate) to One greater than himself, One who was the Promised One of all religions and who would usher in world peace and a new era in religion. The Báb and his followers were opposed and persecuted. In 1850, he was publicly martyred at the age of thirty in Tabríz, Persia. The major Bábí scripture is *The Bayán*.

Bahá'u'lláh - (1817 - 1892 AD) prophet-founder of the Bahá'í Faith. Born on November 12, 1817 in Tehran, Persia, the son of a wealthy government minister, his given name was Mírzá Husayn-'Alíy-i-Núrí. Bahá'u'lláh means "The Glory of God" in Arabic. He declined a career in the government and devoted his life to philanthropic pursuits, earning him renown as the "Father of the Poor." In 1844 he became a Bábí. In 1853, while locked in the *Síyáh-Chál* prison in Tehran (thrown in this notorious "Black Pit" because of his association with the Bábí Faith), he experienced a vision proclaiming that he was the One foretold by The Báb. He suffered persecution, imprisonment and exile for forty years. In April 1863, he declared to his followers in the Garden of *Ridván* (Arabic for Paradise) that he was the Promised One.

NOTES ON THE TEXT

Jalálu'd-Dín Rúmí - (1207 - 1273 AD) a poet who was a follower of Sufi philosophy, a mystical tradition based on Islam. He was born September 30, 1207, Balkh, Afghanistan, which was then part of the Persian empire. He was the founder of the Mawlavi "whirling dervish order." Through prayer and meditation, a Sufi hoped to attained the presence of the Divine.

'Abdu'l-Bahá - (1844 - 1921 AD) son of Bahá'u'lláh, and interpreter and exemplar of his father's teachings. 'Abdu'l-Bahá is Arabic for "the Servant of the Glory." He was his father's closest companion and shared his persecution and suffering in exile. He remained a prisoner until 1908, after which time he travelled extensively, teaching the world-embracing vision of the Bahá'í Faith to the Western world.

The quotations from Bahá'u'lláh (in order of appearance within *The Ink of Light*) are from the following books:

The Hidden Words, page 30 From the Persian #9
The Hidden Words, page 25 From the Arabic #71
Gleanings from the Writings of Bahá'u'lláh, page 160
The Seven Valleys, page 7
Synopsis and Codification of the Kitáb-i-Aqdas, page 27-28
Kitáb-i-Íqán, page 198
The Seven Valleys, page 32
The Seven Valleys, page 36.

The quotations from 'Abdu'l-Bahá (in order of appearance) are from the following books:

Selections from the Writings of 'Abdu'l-Bahá, page 66
Selections from the Writings of 'Abdu'l-Bahá, page 7
Some Answered Questions, page 162-163
Selections from the Writings of 'Abdu'l-Bahá, page 92-93.

The quotations from Jalálu'd-Dín Rúmí are translations (by Marzieh Gail in consultation with Alí-Kulí Khán) appearing in *The Seven Valleys*; however the original source is from Rúmí's *The Mathnavi.*

ACKNOWLEDGEMENTS

The following poems first appeared in journals and anthologies: "november" in *Contemporary Verse 2 (Summer, 1997)*; "A Motion Still," "Nests," and "Her Light" in *Close to the Heart—An Anthology of Canadian Prose and Poetry* (English Garden Publishers, 1996); "the myth of eggs" in *Vintage 96* (Quarry Press, 1997); and "The Body of the World" (titled "The Spirit of Life") in the Bahá'í Poetry Calendar 1996 (White Mountain Publications). "The Ink of Light" and "Consider the human eye" are forthcoming in *Orison VIII.*

My thanks to the editors of those publications.

"Valeska Arriving" was a finalist in the Writers' Union of Canada Postcard Story Competition in 1999.

Special thanks to Eva Tihanyi for her careful reading of the manuscript and her honesty in offering comments and suggestions.

I truly appreciate the guidance and encouragement Don McKay and Janice Kulyk Keefer have given me on the poems about my Ukrainian ancestors, some of which appear in the third section of this book.

Patricia Abram was born and raised in Toronto. She earned a degree in Occupational Therapy from the University of Toronto in 1981 and worked as a paediatric occupational therapist for eight years. In 1989 she moved to St. Catharines, Ontario with her husband and two sons.

In 1995 she served as coeditor of Brock University's literary journal *The Harpweaver,* and as poetry editor in 1996 and 1997. Her poetry has been published in Canadian literary journals, including *The Fiddlehead*, *The Antigonish Review*, *Contemporary Verse 2,* and *Fireweed*, as well as the anthologies *Close to the Heart* (English Garden Publishers, 1996) and *Vintage 96* (Quarry Press, 1997). Her fiction has been published in an anthology of short stories titled *Two Lands: New Visions* (Coteau Books, 1998).